W9-BJF-105

Structures of Life

Developed at

Lawrence Hall of Science

University of California at Berkeley

Published and Distributed by **Delta Education**

ISBN-10: 1-58356-838-7
ISBN-13: 978-1-58356-838-5
542-2008

8 9 10 11 12 13 QUE 14 13 12 11 10 09

TABLE OF CONTENTS

SEEDS ARE EVERYWHERE!

A seed holds the secret of new life. New plants grow from seeds.

Seeds come in many different sizes and shapes. Some are tiny, while others are large and heavy. Some seeds, such as the maple, have wings. Others, such as the creeping thistle, have hairlike tufts. Wings and hairlike tufts act as parachutes to help seeds travel through the air.

Whatever their size or shape, all seeds can become new plants. Seeds start inside flowers. A fruit often grows around the seed to protect it. For example, in the string bean, a pod forms around the seeds. Later the pod breaks, and the seeds fall to the ground. Now they are ready to grow into new plants. This is only one example. Can you think of another?

Walnut

Rice

Corn

Acorns

Strawberry

Wheat

Peas

Squash

1

Seeds as Food

Seeds aren't just for growing new plants. They can also be a source of food!

Many animals eat seeds as part of their diets. Some animals that eat seeds are squirrels, birds, mice, bears, and badgers.

Seeds are an important source of food for people all over the world. Have you ever munched on sunflower seeds or pumpkin seeds? You've probably eaten nuts such as almonds, peanuts, or walnuts. When you eat nuts, you are eating seeds. Anytime you eat grains such as rice, wheat, oats, or corn, you are also eating seeds. Nuts and grains are very healthy for you. They contain vitamins, minerals, carbohydrates, and protein.

A seed grows into the same kind of plant that it came from. When a seed starts to grow, it is called *germination*. First a tiny root breaks out of the seed. The root grows down into the soil. It takes in the water that the new plant needs to grow. Next a shoot or stem grows out of the seed. It grows up, toward the light. Soon leaves will grow on the stem. The seed is now a new plant.

Seeds have three main parts. They are the *embryo*, the *seed coat*, and the *cotyledon*.

Monocot

Dicot

(a) The **embryo** is the part of the seed that grows into a plant. It includes the root, stem, and leaves.

(b) The second part of a seed is the **seed coat**. This tough outer shell protects the seed from injury and keeps it from drying out. The seed coat comes off as the seed begins to germinate.

(c) **Cotyledons** are where food is stored inside the seed. Seeds can have one or two cotyledons. A seed that has one cotyledon, such as corn or barley, is called a **monocot**. A seed that has two cotyledons, such as a bean, is a **dicot**.

Traveling Seeds

Some seeds fall on the ground near the plant. They will grow into new plants there. But it's not good for all the seeds to stay in the same place. If they do, the plants will become crowded and not have enough nutrients or water. So seeds have different ways to travel.

Many seeds are carried to new places by the wind. They can travel many kilometers before they fall to the ground.

Seeds can also be carried to new places by water. If a seed falls into a stream, the rushing water may carry it to a new spot downstream. Sometimes a heavy rain may wash a seed to a new spot. The most famous water traveler is the coconut. The outer coat of a coconut is waterproof. Inside this coat are air and fibers that help the coconut float. Deep inside the coconut is the seed of a new plant. Coconuts fall from trees when they are ripe. Sometimes they roll into the water, and the water carries them to new places. After a while, the waterproof coat wears away. Then the seed can sprout into a new plant.

Animals spread seeds, too. Squirrels bury acorns, hickory nuts, and peanuts to eat during the winter. But they never find all the seeds they bury. Some of the seeds they miss grow into new plants. Many fruits are eaten by birds and other animals. The seeds in the fruits pass through the animals' digestive systems. Then the seeds leave the animals' bodies in their droppings.

Some seeds have sharp hooks or burrs that can stick to an animal's fur or a person's clothes. This is another way seeds travel to new places.

A red squirrel feeding in winter

3

THE MOST IMPORTANT SEED

Rice must have very wet, warm conditions to grow.

Did you know that a kind of grass seed is the main food source for almost half the people in the world? This food is rice.

Rice was one of the first crops to be *cultivated,* or grown. In fact, it has been cultivated in Asia for at least 8,000 years!

Rice is grown in many parts of the world. The largest producers are China and India. The United States, Europe, and Australia grow rice, too.

Rice is grown in flooded fields called *paddies.* The paddy is flooded either by rain or by irrigation. Then seeds are sown in the flooded field. Flooding gives rice the moisture it needs to grow. It also kills weeds and pests that might harm the plants. The field is kept underwater until 2 or 3 weeks

4

before the rice is ready to be picked. Then the paddy is drained, and the rice is harvested. It takes about 6 months for rice to grow.

In the United States, rice farmers use airplanes to sow the rice seeds. When the rice is ready to be harvested, a huge machine called a *combine* does the job. But in some parts of the world, people do the work by hand. Often they use animals to help them. Oxen and water buffalo are used in Asia to pull simple harvesting machines.

Oxen plowing a rice paddy in Asia

Have you heard of white rice and brown rice? These types of rice got their names because of their colors. Brown rice is brown because it includes *bran.* Bran is the hard outer covering of a grain. White rice has the bran removed. Brown rice has more vitamins and fiber than white rice.

Rice is cooked in many ways around the world. In Italy, it is eaten as *risotto,* a creamy mix of rice, cheese, and vegetables. In Japan, raw fish is served with sticky rice to make *sushi.* Spanish people enjoy *paella*, rice mixed with meat, seafood, vegetables, and spices. British people and Americans enjoy rice pudding for dessert. Many Americans eat toasted rice cereals for breakfast or sweetened, crispy rice cakes as snacks. Any way you make it, rice is good for you!

Varieties of Rice

There are at least 1,300 types of rice. Each has its own shape, color, and flavor.

Some rice is called *long-grain*. Long-grain rice is dry and fluffy when it is cooked. Other rice is *short-grain*. Short-grain rice is stickier than long-grain rice. However, there is no nutritional difference.

BARBARA McCLINTOCK

Did you ever believe strongly in something? Even if everyone told you your idea was silly or just plain wrong? A scientist named Barbara McClintock faced that problem for much of her life. But she never stopped believing in what she knew was true.

Barbara McClintock was born in Hartford, Connecticut, in 1902. Even when she was little, Barbara liked to do things her own way. She enjoyed all kinds of sports. Her favorite pastime was playing baseball with the boys in the neighborhood. Barbara was the only girl on the boys' team. She knew that the boys didn't really want her to play with them. But Barbara didn't care what other people thought. She kept on playing because she wanted to play.

Barbara's parents didn't mind that she acted differently from most other girls of that time. They supported her in just about everything she wanted to do.

Barbara McClintock

Barbara also did well in school. When she graduated from high school, she wanted to go to college. In those days, most girls did not go to college. But Barbara's father agreed that she should go. Barbara quickly enrolled in the College of Agriculture at Cornell University in Ithaca, New York. There she studied plants and how to grow them.

Barbara loved college life. She played in a jazz band. She was president of the freshman women. Barbara loved studying, too. After a while, she began to focus on her studies. She became especially interested in the field of *genetics*.

Barbara decided to become a *geneticist*. A geneticist is a scientist who studies how traits are passed on from one generation to the next. Barbara spent most of her time studying the traits of corn. She studied its color, size, and texture.

An ear of corn

She grew fields of corn and studied the corn kernels. By studying them, she could tell what traits were passed down through a corn's seeds.

Despite her hard work, McClintock found it hard to get a job when she graduated from Cornell in 1927. In those days, women were not taken seriously as scientists. She taught at Cornell for a while. However, the school would not give a woman a permanent job. McClintock then did research and taught at several other colleges.

What Is Genetics?

Genetics is the study of how living things pass certain *traits*, or qualities, to their offspring. A trait that is passed down from generation to generation is called an *inherited trait*. For example, people with brown eyes will probably have a child with brown eyes.

In 1931, McClintock made an important discovery. Scientists already knew that every living thing contains bundles of messages that tell what kind of animal or plant it is and what it should look like. These bundles are called *chromosomes*, and the messages are called *genes*. Scientists thought that if a gene was located on a certain chromosome, it would always be there. But McClintock discovered that this was not true. She did many experiments. These experiments showed her that genes could *cross over*, or move, from one chromosome to another. Crossing over meant that a greater variety of traits could exist.

McClintock often ignored the rules of the schools where she worked. If her summer corn crop wasn't ready when school started in the fall, she didn't report to work. She was

Harvesting a corn field

impatient with anyone who didn't understand her work. She also spoke out often about the lack of opportunity for women scientists.

In 1941, McClintock got a research position at the Cold Spring Harbor Laboratory on Long Island in New York. She stayed there for the rest of her life. At the Cold Spring Harbor lab, McClintock was free to do the research she loved. She often worked 80 hours a week.

McClintock presented some of her findings at a meeting in 1951. In 1952, she published a paper about her work. But nobody listened to her! Most people didn't understand what McClintock was talking about. Others simply didn't believe her. At first, McClintock was disappointed and surprised at the reaction she got. But she soon went back to work. Once again, she didn't care what other people thought. She knew she was right.

Although McClintock won several awards, her work still wasn't widely appreciated. That began to change in the 1970s. By then, scientists were able to use new technology to study McClintock's ideas. They proved what she had known to be true since 1951. It had been more than 25 years since she had first talked about her ideas.

Finally McClintock's theories were accepted by other scientists. She received many honors and awards. In 1983, at the age of 81, she received the Nobel Prize for Physiology or Medicine.

Barbara McClintock continued working until her death in 1992 at the age of 90. She was always very independent and sure of herself. And she was never bitter about all the years she was ignored. "If you know you're right, you don't care," she said.

King Gustav of Sweden presents the Nobel prize to Barbara McClintock.

QUESTIONS TO EXPLORE

- What are some of the things that made Barbara McClintock a good scientist?
- Why do you think it took so long for McClintock's ideas to be accepted?
- If you could ask Barbara McClintock a question about her work, what would you ask?

HYDRO-GROWING

You've probably seen a plant in a garden or a flowerpot. Plants in gardens and flowerpots grow in soil. The soil provides nutrients for the plants. But did you know that plants can be grown without soil? Raising plants without soil is called *hydroponics*.

Hydroponics is not new. It was first developed back in the mid-1800s. Hydroponics became popular during the 1930s. At that time, scientists were experimenting to find different ways to provide nutrition to plants.

There are two main types of hydroponics. One is called *water culture*. The other is *aggregate culture*. In both methods, seeds sprout and grow just as they would if they were planted in soil. But hydroponic gardens look very different than regular gardens!

In water culture, the plants are grown with their roots in the water. This water contains nutrients. The roots absorb the water and nutrients. But because there is no soil, the roots cannot hold the plant up as they would in the ground. Instead the plants must be supported from above by metal rods.

In aggregate culture, the plants' roots are placed in sand or gravel. This helps the roots hold up the plant. A solution containing nutrients is placed in the sand or gravel. This solution is either pumped from below or sprayed from above.

Why would you want to grow plants without soil? One reason is that hydroponics

Seedy Facts
Did you know...?

■ The biggest seed is the fruit of the great fan palm. It can weigh as much as 20 kilograms (44 pounds). This seed is commonly known as the double coconut. It grows wild in the Seychelles Islands in the Indian Ocean.

■ The smallest seeds are from a type of tropical orchid. One billion seeds weigh just 1 gram.

■ In July 1954, some Arctic lupine seeds were found frozen at Miller Creek in the Yukon Territory of Canada. In 1966, these seeds were planted. The seeds grew into plants. Scientists later discovered the seeds were probably from around 13,000 B.C.E. That means they were almost 15,000 years old!

Tomatoes grown in aggregate

Flowers hydroponically cultivated at Lake Inle in Burma

helps scientists study plants. Scientists can change the amounts and types of nutrients to see what combinations make the plants grow best.

Hydroponics is also a good way to grow plants in areas where the soil isn't right for plants. For example, hydroponics has been used to grow tomatoes and cucumbers in the deserts of Arab countries. Hydroponics can also be used in places where there is no soil at all. Plants can be grown on ships or in ice-covered areas such as Antarctica. They could even be grown in space stations hundreds of kilometers from Earth! Hydroponics is a great example of how high-tech methods can make something as simple as planting a seed work in a whole new way.

SEEDING SPACE

March 5, 2132

Katie Lin sighed as she looked out the sealed window of her bedroom. Outside was a beautiful view of a black sky filled with thousands of stars. But Katie didn't want to see stars. She wanted to see grass and trees. She wanted to see Earth.

Katie and her parents had arrived at the New World Space Center on the planet Mars just a few days ago. Everyone there was very nice. But it just didn't feel like home to Katie. Instead of a house, she and her parents lived in a few small rooms. Instead of playing baseball on an outdoor field, Katie saw children playing inside on a playground. Worst of all, there were no smells of flowers growing and no pretty gardens to look at. Back on Earth, Katie had tended plants in a garden with her father. But in the days since she had arrived at New World, she hadn't seen anything green except for the spinach on her plate at dinner.

Katie heard a tap on her door. "Hi, Katie. Are you all right?" asked Dan Mesa. Dan sat next to Katie in school and had been pretty friendly.

"I'm okay," Katie said. She tried to smile. "I'm just feeling a little homesick."

"I know what you mean," Dan said. "When my family arrived here last year, I couldn't sleep for a week! But there's lots of fun things to do here. What do you miss most about Earth?"

"Gardens," Katie said right away. "I can't get used to a place where there are no plants or flowers."

"But there are plants here!" Dan said in surprise. "There's a whole garden over on the other side of the space center. Come on and I'll show you."

Katie didn't have to be asked twice. In a flash, she was on her feet and following Dan down the hall. The two walked until they came to a door marked *Hydroponics Lab.*

"Hydroponics Lab?" Katie said. "That doesn't sound like a garden to me."

"Just look," Dan said. He opened the door, and they stepped inside.

Katie couldn't believe her eyes. The room was filled with tanks. Each tank held several plants. Some of them looked just like the plants Katie had grown at home. Others were completely different.

Katie stepped up to a tank for a closer look. "What kind of garden is this?" she asked. The little plants were held up by thin metal rods. The tanks were filled with water, not soil. Katie could even see the roots of the plants.

"I don't get it," Katie said. "How can plants grow without any soil? Why are there pieces of metal holding up the plants? And what's that noise?" The air was filled with the hum of machines and the gurgle of bubbling water.

"We don't need soil to grow plants in a hydroponic garden," Dan explained. "These plants grow in water. *Hydro* means water." He pointed to a machine next to the tank. "That humming noise is coming from pumps like this. They pump air and nutrients into the tanks."

"Why?" Katie asked. "My garden at home didn't have a pump."

Dan didn't answer her right away. Instead he waved at a boy and a girl standing near the tanks on the next table. "There are Peter and Latifah. They're doing a project on hydroponics for school. Let's ask them all about it."

Katie and Dan joined the others. "Katie's never seen a hydroponic garden before," Dan explained. "She wants to know how we can grow plants without soil."

Peter smiled. "Even though we don't have any good soil on Mars, it's still important to have plants up here. Plants provide food for us to eat."

"Like spinach," Katie said, remembering dinner.

"Plants provide oxygen, too," Dan added. "Plants release oxygen into the air. People and animals need that oxygen to breathe."

"Right," Peter agreed. "So we have to grow plants without soil. Soil does two things for a plant. It provides nutrients, and it holds the roots so the plant can stand up. We don't have any soil here. But we do have water and nutrients. So we add nutrients to the water and grow the plants that way."

Katie pointed at the metal rods holding up each plant. "And since there's no soil to hold up the plants, those rods do the job and help the plant grow up straight?"

"Yes!" said Latifah. "Hydroponics is the best way to grow plants in space. After all, it would be hard to have a lot of land inside a space station!"

"It still seems weird to grow plants in water rather than soil," Katie complained.

"Take a look at this," Dan said. The group walked over to a table filled with more tanks. But these tanks were filled with gravel. "This is another type of hydroponic gardening. Instead of soil, we use gravel or sand to hold up the plants. A pump floods the gravel with water and nutrients so the plants can grow."

"Which system works better?" Katie asked.

"They both work about the same," Peter told her. "Using gravel works better to grow lots of plants for us to use for food. But suspending the plants in water is the better way to do experiments."

Once again, Katie was surprised. "Plant experiments?"

"Sure!" Latifah said. "In fact, Peter and I have an experiment going right here." She pointed to three hydroponic tanks. The plants in the first and last tanks looked a lot healthier than the ones in the center tank.

"Those plants don't look so good," Katie said, pointing to the center tank. "What's going on?"

"The plants in the first tank are getting distilled water with added nutrients," Latifah explained. "The water is clean. The plants that look weak and sick are getting water recycled from the laundry. Used water is called *gray water.* It looks like the gray water isn't good for growing these plants."

"What about the third tank?" Katie asked.

"Those plants are also getting gray water. But that gray water has been filtered to purify it. We want to find out whether cleaning the water can make it as good for plants as distilled water."

Katie wandered over to look at the shelves against the wall. They were filled with boxes of different nutrients. "What's all this?" she asked.

"Those are the nutrients we add to the water," Peter said.

"Is that sort of like adding fertilizer to plants on Earth to help them grow stronger?" Katie asked.

"Exactly," Latifah agreed. "Fertilizer is full of nutrients."

Katie reached out and touched the leaf of a plant. "This is so neat! I never imagined there could be gardens in space."

Latifah hurried away and came back carrying an empty tank the size of a fish tank. "Here, Katie," she said. "We'll help you start your own hydroponic garden. You can grow anything you want!"

Katie smiled for the first time in days. Maybe life on Mars wouldn't be so different from Earth after all!

QUESTIONS TO EXPLORE

- What are the different kinds of hydroponics that might be used in space?
- What are the advantages and disadvantages of each kind of hydroponics?
- If you were living in space, what hydroponic system would you use? What plants would you grow?

ANSWERING KIDS' QUESTIONS:
CRAYFISH, CRAWFISH, CRAWDADDY

Lobster

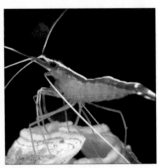
Shrimp

Crab

Crayfish

How do you think it would feel to have your skeleton on the outside of your body? Most animals on Earth do! One group of animals with their skeletons on the outside is called *crustaceans*. Crustaceans include lobsters, shrimp, crabs, and crayfish. A crayfish is about 5 to 12.5 centimeters (2 to 5 inches) long. Crayfish come in several colors. They can be red, brown, or gray-brown.

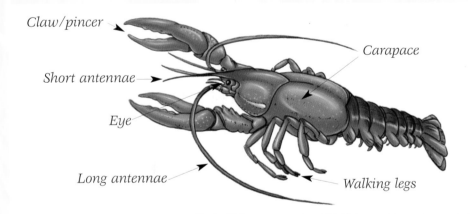

Claw/pincer
Short antennae
Eye
Long antennae
Carapace
Walking legs

Q: What does a crayfish look like?

A: A crayfish has five pairs of legs. The first pair, near the crayfish's head, has strong claws. The crayfish uses these claws for eating, defending itself from other crayfish, and burrowing into the ground.

A crayfish has two eyes. They are mounted on stalks sticking out from the crayfish's head. These eyes can turn and see in any direction. Two pairs of antennae can also be found on the crayfish's head. These antennae help the crayfish sense movement and feel its way around.

A crayfish's body has a hard covering. This covering is an outer skeleton called the *exoskeleton*. It protects the crayfish from harm, just like a suit of armor protected a knight in battle. A crayfish's skeleton is very different from yours. Your skeleton is inside your body. As your body gets bigger, so does your skeleton. A crayfish's skeleton is on the outside of its body and cannot grow. The crayfish grows a new, soft skeleton inside the old, hard one, then sheds the older one. The crayfish immediately grows into the new, soft skeleton. After a few days, the new skeleton hardens. This process is called *molting*.

The crayfish's skeleton can grow new parts. If a crayfish's leg or claw is broken off, a new one will grow the next time the crayfish molts.

Q: What do crayfish eat?

A: Crayfish eat a lot of different things. They eat insects, worms, snails, frog eggs, and small fish. They also eat dead plants and animals they find in the water. This helps keep the water clean.

A crayfish eats by holding its food in one of its front claws. It bites off bits of food, then swallows them.

Crayfish don't only eat. They also are eaten! Many animals eat crayfish, including raccoons, large fish, turtles, snakes, and birds.

People like to eat crayfish, too. In fact, this little animal is a big part of people's diets. This is especially true in the southern part of the United States. There are even large farms that raise crayfish to be sold to stores and restaurants. Crayfish can be cooked in many different ways. They can be fried, boiled, or used in stews and casseroles.

Q: Where do crayfish live?

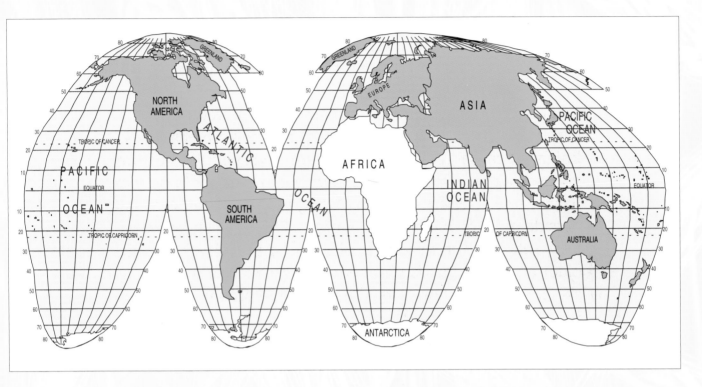

A: Crayfish live on every continent except Africa and Antarctica. There are 200 species of crayfish in North America.

Most crayfish live in fresh water. Ponds and streams where the water is not too hot or too cold make good *habitats,* or places to live. Crayfish live on the bottoms of ponds or near the banks of streams where they can find shelter. They burrow into the mud, hide under rocks, or hide in plants.

A Crayfish by Any Other Name

Did you know that crayfish have many names? They are called *crawfish, crawdaddies, crawdads, crabs,* and *mudbugs.* Crayfish have special scientific names in Latin, too. For example, one kind of crayfish found in North America is called *Procambarus clarki.*

LIFE CYCLE OF A CRAYFISH

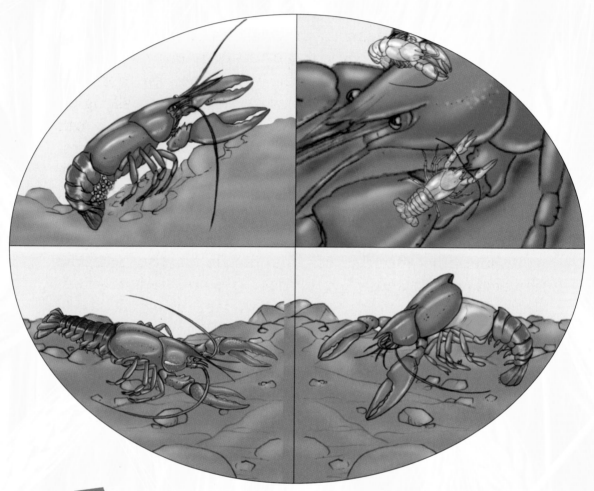

A crayfish starts its life as an egg. When the egg hatches, the crayfish is very tiny. But it is fully formed and looks just like an adult. The baby crayfish stays with its mother for 1 or 2 weeks. During those weeks, it never wanders far from its mother. If it is frightened by something, it moves very quickly, clinging to the underside of its mother for protection. In 2 weeks, it is about 1 centimeter (one-half inch) long. It leaves its mother and heads out for life on its own. The average life span of a crayfish is 3 to 8 years.

Young crayfish grow very fast. As they grow, they molt often and grow new exoskeletons. For a day or two after each molt, the new skeleton is soft. Because a crayfish with a new, soft skeleton is easy for a predator to catch and eat, the crayfish stays out of sight. It hides in the mud, under plants, or under rocks until its skeleton is hard and strong.

Crayfish reach their adult size when they are just 3 or 4 months old. They spend their lives at the bottoms of ponds or along the banks of streams. A crayfish digs a home in the mud. Their homes can be up to a meter (3.3 feet) long!

Although crayfish live in the water, they are not good swimmers. Most of the time, they get around by walking on the four pairs of legs behind the front claws. Crayfish can move surprisingly fast. They can move forward, backward, and sideways. If a crayfish needs to escape danger, its body darts backward with a quick snap of its tail. A crayfish will raise its front claws to fight if it is attacked. A pinch from those claws can really hurt!

Some time after the male and female crayfish mate, the female lays hundreds of eggs. These eggs aren't left in a nest. Instead they stick to the swimmerets under the female's body and tail. She carries them around. When they hatch, a new generation of crayfish is born.

The story of a crayfish, from egg through growth to producing new eggs, is a story that repeats over and over again. Scientists call this story the *life cycle* of the crayfish.

A crayfish with its claws raised

LIFE ON EARTH

The diversity of life on Earth is amazing. Plants and animals live in every *environment* imaginable. They live in oceans, on mountains, in wetlands, and every place else. Some environments are hot, some are wet, and some are very cold. The conditions in an environment determine what organisms can and can't live there. Plants and animals that live in a pond can't live in a grassland. Plants and animals that live in a grassland can't live in the ocean. Plants and animals have structures that help them grow, survive, and *reproduce* in their environments.

CALIFORNIA CENTRAL VALLEY WETLANDS

The central valley of California has lots of wetlands. *Wetlands* are places with ponds, streams, swamps, and muddy fields. Cattails and other plants grow in the water, and cottonwood and willow trees line the ponds and streams.

California central valley wetlands

In many wetlands, cattails are the most successful plants. The strong roots hold tightly to the bottoms of ponds. The brown hot dog–shaped structures are seed heads. Each seed head has thousands of seeds, able to reproduce thousands of cattail plants.

Lots of animals live in the water. Crayfish live on the bottoms of ponds. Their hard shells and strong pincers help them defend themselves from *predators*. Their wide tails let them swim away quickly. The females' long swimmerets let them carry their eggs safely to improve chances of reproduction. When it's time to grow, crayfish molt their old shell. The new shell is soft for about a day. The crayfish grow before the new shell hardens.

A catfish

A bullfrog

Other animals share ponds with crayfish. Catfish swim around in the water. They look for insects and bits of plants to eat. Their fins let them move easily through water. They have two sharp spines on their sides for defense. Catfish live their whole lives in the water.

Bullfrogs live on the edges of the ponds. They have long, sticky tongues for capturing large insects like dragonflies. They have strong legs for jumping and webbed feet for swimming. Bullfrogs escape into the water if a land predator comes by.

Raccoons live in the trees and willows in the wetlands. They come down to the ponds to look for food. They might catch a frog or crayfish, or find a bird's nest with eggs. Their handlike front feet and sharp teeth allow them to eat many different things.

Each fall the wetlands have visitors that stay from October to April. They are the thousands of ducks, geese, and cranes that fly south from their breeding grounds in Canada and Alaska. They are known as *waterfowl*. The highway in the air that they follow is the Pacific flyway.

A raccoon

Geese and ducks in wetlands

The wetlands provide food and safety for waterfowl during the winter. They swim calmly on the ponds and fly out to the fields to eat seeds. The weather is mild, and there are few predators. As long as the wetlands get enough water to fill the ponds and flood the fields, waterfowl will continue to *thrive* in California's central valley.

MOJAVE DESERT

California's deserts are very different from the wetlands. The Mojave Desert in southern California is dry, often hot, and rocky. Desert plants have structures for getting and holding water. Cactuses have thick stems to store water. Desert trees have small, waxy leaves to conserve water.

Mojave Desert

Desert animals need to get water, too. Kangaroo rats and desert tortoises get water from the seeds, leaves, and flowers they eat. These two desert animals rarely need to drink water. Cactus wrens can fly to water for a drink. Desert coyotes can travel long distances on long legs to get water.

A cactus wren

A coyote

A tortoise

FORESTS

Yosemite National Park in central California is one of the most beautiful mountain parks in the world. Pine, fir, and oak trees thrive in the mountain environment. The park is cold in the winter and warm in the summer. The forest trees must be able to survive months of cold winter with deep snow on the ground.

A pine and fir forest in the mountains

The snowshoe hare lives in the forest all year. In winter, it grows white fur. The white fur blends in with the white snow making it hard to see. This adaption improves the hare's chance of survival. The sharp-eyed owl can only spot the hare when it moves. The owl's sharp talons and strong beak allow it to catch the hare for a meal.

A snowshoe hare

A great horned owl

The black bear has strong claws for digging up roots and tearing apart dead trees to find food. When winter comes, the bear finds a den for safety. It will sleep through the winter, living off its layer of fat. In the spring, when the snow is gone, the bear comes out to feed on the fresh berries and plants.

A black bear

A mule deer

Deer are the fastest-running animals in the forest. They are always alert for danger as they nibble grass and twigs for food. When they sense danger, they can run away in a flash. Deer leave the high forest in the winter and move to lower areas where they can find food.

GRASSLANDS

The prairie and the Great Plains of North America are grasslands. As you might guess, grasses are the main plants growing there. Few trees and bushes grow in the grasslands. Range fires often sweep across the grasslands, burning the dry grass and small trees. Grass plants are not killed by fire. They can grow new blades from their underground roots in the spring. Many other plants cannot survive fire. This is how the grasslands stay the way they are.

A grassland

Many animals live in the sea of grass. Prairie dogs have strong legs and claws for digging large networks of tunnels underground. They come out to eat the grass. Grasshoppers live right in the grass. They hop and fly from place to place to get food. American bison wander across the grassland, eating the grass as they go. Horned larks are seasonal visitors. They fly to the grasslands in the summer to feed on grass seeds and raise their young. In the winter, they fly south where it is warmer.

A prairie dog

A grasshopper

A bison

A horned lark

Fire is a challenge for animals living in the grassland environment. Large animals like bison can move to a new location to escape the fire. Prairie dogs can retreat into their tunnels. Horned larks can fly away. But if they have eggs in a nest, or babies that can't yet fly, they will die. The grasshoppers are not strong fliers. They can fly a short distance to safety, but if the fire is large, the grasshoppers will die.

In the spring after a fire, new grass sprouts come up from the roots. The ashes provide nutrients for the new grass. The animals that ran from the fire will return. Grasshoppers will fly in and reproduce. The grassland is soon full of life once again.

TUNDRA

Tundra is cold, frozen land most of the year. Northern Alaska is tundra. During the winter, the ground is frozen. Days are short. Plants stop growing, and most animals seek shelter from snow and wind.

Tundra

Only animals with thick fur or feathers can survive the tundra winters. Arctic foxes scavenge for scraps of food. Ptarmigans scratch through snow to find seeds and plant buds. Foxes and ptarmigan grow white fur and feathers in winter. They blend in with the white environment.

A ptarmigan

An arctic fox

In the summer, days are long, the weather is warm, and the soil defrosts. The tundra comes to life. Countless millions of mosquitoes swarm over the pools and marshes where they reproduce. Millions of birds come to the summer tundra to raise their young. This is when the snowy owl of the tundra raises its young as well. The owl catches mice and voles to feed its young. It also catches baby birds and fish from time to time.

A mosquito swarm

The tundra goes through big changes in weather over the year. Animals that don't have structures to protect them from the cold have to leave. Those that don't leave will freeze to death when conditions change.

A snowy owl

OCEANS

More than half of Earth's surface is seawater. Ocean water is cold in the far north and far south, and warm in the middle parts of the planet. The warm oceans are called *tropical oceans*.

A tropical ocean

Life on the land is based on plants. But there are no plants in the tropical oceans. The tropical oceans are known for the diversity of their animals. The most important animals in this tropical ocean are the corals. They surround themselves with hard shell for protection. In this way, they build huge structures called *reefs*. Thousands of animals make their homes in the coral reef environment.

The coral animals change their environment. They build huge reefs that provide lots of places for other animals to grow, hide, and find food. The reef benefits animals that need a surface to stick to, like snails and clams. The reef benefits animals that need places to hide, like shrimps and lobsters.

The reef provides a resting place for ocean travelers like the green sea turtle. This turtle is being groomed by a small school of fish. The turtle lies quietly as the fish eat *parasites* that attach to the turtle.

A green sea turtle on a coral reef

A CHANGE IN THE ENVIRONMENT

All plants and animals change the environments in which they live. Trees create shade. Flowers produce odors. Ground squirrels dig tunnels in the soil. Woodpeckers drill holes in trees. And every animal eats something. Most of the changes to the environment are small. The plants and animals living there continue to go about their business.

Some animals, however, change their environments a lot. As a result, many plants and animals living in the environment must move or they will die. One animal that makes big changes to its environment is the beaver.

A beaver cutting down a tree

Beavers live in water. They build a mud and stick lodge right in the water. The entrance to the lodge is underwater. The place where they live is above water. Beavers are safe and comfortable in their lodges.

If a lake or pond is nearby, the beaver family makes its lodge there. If there is only a stream, the beavers go to work to make a pond. First they use their large, sharp front teeth to cut down trees by the stream.

An adult beaver and its young

They cut off the branches and drag them into the stream. They put mud and rocks on the branches to hold them in place. Then they add more branches and mud. The beavers are making a dam.

The beavers keep adding to the dam until it reaches all the way across the stream. Water backs up behind the dam, forming a pond. The beavers then build their lodge.

A beaver dam

But what about the plants and other animals living in the stream environment? Some of them benefit from the beaver's work. Others can't live there any more.

The beavers cut down the trees for food and building material. This means less shade. When water floods the land around the stream, the grasses, bushes, and trees living there die. Insects, snakes, squirrels, and all the other land animals have to move out. The plants and animals that live on land lose when the beavers build a pond.

It's a different story for the water plants and animals. Fish and frogs have a lot more room to live. Water plants, like cattails and water lilies, thrive. Water insects, like dragonflies and mosquitoes, benefit from the changed environment. Water plants and animals grow and reproduce to take advantage of the larger environment created by the beavers.

A SNAIL'S JOURNEY

The snail wanted to find a new home. It needed a home where there were cool, damp places to hide. The new home also had to have leaves and plants for the snail to eat.

The snail set out on a cool spring morning, before the sun was up. The grass was damp with dew. The snail moved by using the muscular "foot" on its belly. As it crawled along the ground, the snail left a trail of slimy mucus. The mucus helped the snail slide over the ground.

As the snail crawled, the sun slowly rose in the sky. Suddenly a bird swooped down. Quickly the snail pulled its body inside its hard shell. It sensed the bird's beak banging against the top of its shell, but the bird could not break the shell. The bird soon flew away. When all was safe, the snail poked its head and foot out of its shell and continued its journey.

Soon the sun grew warmer, and the grass began to dry and get hot. The snail could not stay out in such conditions. If it did, its body would dry up, and it would die.

The snail crawled toward a shady spot under a tree. It found some mushrooms growing where the ground was cool and damp. The snail settled under a mushroom, pulled its body into its shell, and rested.

When the snail poked its head out of its shell again, it was dark and the air was cool. The snail crawled along until it found some leaves. Then it began to rub its tongue across the leaves. Thousands of sharp teeth on its tongue ripped up bits of the leaves for the snail to swallow.

The snail traveled for many days looking for its new home. It usually traveled early in the morning or during the night. Cloudy days were good, too, because the sun didn't make the snail too hot. But there were other dangers besides the sun to worry about.

One night, a raccoon tried to eat the snail. It hit the snail with its paw. The snail quickly slipped inside its shell. The

raccoon picked up the shell and shook it, trying to get the animal to come out. But a strong muscle held the snail in its shell. After a while, the raccoon gave up.

Finally the snail crawled into a garden. There were tasty plants to eat. There were a lot of damp places to hide, such as the roots of a shady tree, a patch of mushrooms, and a jumble of rocks. Salamanders were hiding under the rocks, and grass frogs hopped around the garden. Earthworms tunneled through the soil, making it a good place for plants to grow. Beetles crawled through the dirt. The snail settled down under a leaf and began to eat. It was home at last!

Inside a Snail's Shell

A snail has many of the same body parts as you, but they are in different places! Its teeth are on its tongue. A snail's toothy tongue is called a *radula*. Did you know a snail's mouth is on its foot? And its breathing hole is next to where it excretes waste!

A common garden snail

A snail has several tentacles on its head. Its eyes are at the ends of the two longer tentacles. A snail doesn't have very good eyesight, but it can tell light from dark.

A snail also uses its tentacles to feel its way around. Scent detectors on the tentacles help the snail find food to eat and tell the snail when other animals are close by.

A snail's foot is covered with tiny hairs called *cilia*. These help the foot grip the ground. A special gland in the snail's foot produces a thick trail of slime to help it slide along.

A snail's hard shell protects it from predators. It also gives the snail a safe place to stay when it's hot and dry outside. The shell becomes thicker and harder as the snail grows. It coils around the snail's body as it grows.

Jeweltop snails

Basic Snail Facts

- Snails have shells. Their close relatives, the slugs, do not. The shell is the only difference between the two creatures.
- Snails are part of the family called *gastropods.* That word is from two Greek words that mean "belly-foot."
- A snail's tongue can have as many as 150,000 teeth!
- Snails produce slime to help them move.
- A snail makes its shell bigger by adding new material to the opening of the shell.
- There are about 40,000 different types of snails.
- Snails live on land and in the water.
- The largest land snail is found in Africa. Its shell is almost 27.5 centimeters (11 inches) long!
- Most land snails are both male and female. That means any snail can fertilize the eggs of any other snail.
- Snails lay about 30 to 50 tiny eggs into a hole. Because the snail doesn't stay to protect the eggs, many are eaten by insects.
- A snail's shell grows for the first 2 years of a snail's life. By then, the shell can have four or five coils.
- Snails are right-handed or left-handed! If a snail's shell coils to the right, it is right-handed. A left-handed snail has a shell that coils to the left.
- Most snails live about 3 or 4 years.
- Snails hibernate in the winter. They seal the openings of their shells with thick plugs of slime to keep their bodies wet as they sleep.

Snail shells

CRAYFISH, SNAILS, AND KIDS

There are many similarities between a crayfish, a snail, and you! There are many differences, too. Let's take a look at what is the same and what is different.

SKELETON

A crayfish's skeleton is on the outside of its body. It protects the crayfish from predators and other dangers. This exoskeleton doesn't grow along with the crayfish. The crayfish has to shed its too-small shell to grow. A crayfish can also grow a new leg or claw if the old one breaks off.

A snail has an outer shell that protects it from predators, too. A snail's shell grows along with the snail's body for the first 2 years of its life. The snail never sheds its shell. If a snail's shell cracks or breaks, it does not grow a new one.

Your skeleton is inside your body. It provides structure, gives your body shape, protects your internal organs, and allows for movement. Your skeleton keeps growing along with you. You can't grow a new arm or leg, but if you break a bone, new bone tissue will usually grow in to heal the injury.

INTERNAL ORGANS

Crayfish, snails, and humans all have a heart to pump blood. They all have a stomach to digest food and glands to excrete wastes.

Humans and snails that live on land have lungs to breathe air. Crayfish usually live in the water. Instead of using lungs to breathe, they get their oxygen out of the water through gills. The gills are tucked up under the carapace where the legs attach to the body.

What structures are similar on humans, snails, and crayfish? What structures are different?

LIMBS

Crayfish have five pairs of legs. They can walk quickly in any direction on four of these pairs. This helps them move along the bottoms of ponds or streams as they look for food or avoid predators. The fifth pair of legs, located near the head, has large claws. These claws are more like arms than legs. The crayfish uses them to pick up food and defend itself against predators.

Snails have no arms or legs. A snail moves with a muscular foot on the bottom of its body. This foot allows the snail to crawl over almost any surface.

Humans have two legs to walk, run, and climb. They have two arms to pick up things and carry them.

THE FOOD WEB

Every animal depends on other animals or plants to survive. To survive, every living thing needs energy. The Sun provides energy for plants. Animals get energy by eating plants and other animals. This network is called the *food web.*

A food web starts with the energy the Sun gives to plants. Plants are the primary source of matter in a food web. They provide energy to *herbivores,* animals that eat plants. Herbivores are then eaten by *carnivores,* or meat-eaters. The diagram shows an example of a food web.

Crayfish, snails, and humans are parts of food webs, too. Humans eat animals such as chickens, pigs, cattle, and fish. People who do not eat meat or fish eat plant materials such as vegetables, fruits, and grains.

Crayfish and snails are sources of food for humans. In fact, both crayfish and snails are raised on farms that provide food for people around the world.

An example of a food web that includes the crayfish

QUESTIONS TO EXPLORE

■ **Can you describe or draw a group of animals in a food web?**

■ **Can you tell about another food web?**

■ **Where do you fit into a food web?**

A CHANCE ENCOUNTER

CRAYFISH: Hey, Slimy, how are you tonight?

SNAIL: I had a rough day. The kids were watching me do all sorts of things today.

CRAYFISH: You mean you got to experiment with the kids? That sounds fun!

SNAIL: You think it's fun to be picked up and moved around? First they weighed me and measured how long I was. Then they had me pull these silver rings around to see how strong I was. After that, they put me on a desk and wrote down how long it took me to crawl from one end to the other. I'm exhausted! All I want to do is eat some lettuce and go to sleep.

CRAYFISH: Don't be such a grouch! The kids like to observe what I can do, too. It's not so bad. Anyway, we're doing important work!

SNAIL: We are?

CRAYFISH: Sure! We're helping these kids be scientists. Each activity helps the kids learn. And the more people know about us animals and how we live, the more they'll want to take care of this planet and keep it a nice place to live.

SNAIL: I never thought of it like that. This classroom *is* a pretty nice place to live. I always have plenty of food.

CRAYFISH: And it's nice that the kids clean our tanks and give us fresh water.

SNAIL: I guess this isn't such a bad life after all!

LIFE IN LOS ANGELES

Thirty thousand years ago people did not live in California. But animals did. They roamed across the part of southern California where the city of Los Angeles is now. Some of the animals were the same ones you might see in California today, like coyotes, mountain lions, and black bears. But some of the animals that were alive then are gone today. How do we know they were in California 30,000 years ago?

Not far from downtown Los Angeles is a place called the La Brea tar pits. The area has a lot of pools of hard, black tar. In the summer heat, the tar melts.

When animals stepped into the melted tar thousands of years ago, they got stuck. They couldn't get out. Slowly they sank into the sticky goo and died.

A tar pit at La Brea

In 1901 scientists discovered that the tar pits were full of bones. When they dug the bones out of the tar, they found some bones that were unlike any they had seen before. They carefully put the bones together. Some of the skeletons they saw were of *extinct* animals.

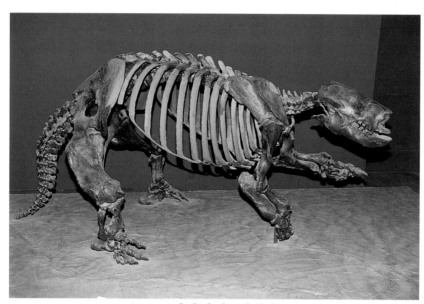

A ground sloth fossil skeleton

Thirty thousand years ago ground sloths were common in southern California. But ground sloths are extinct now. Scientists discovered that ground sloths lived in California when they found their bones in the tar pits. They are similar to tree sloths found in the rain forests of South America.

A painting of what a ground sloth may have looked like

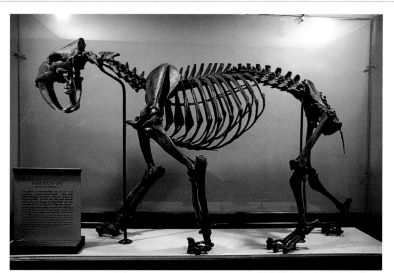

A saber-toothed cat fossil skeleton

Saber-toothed cats no longer live on Earth. They were similar to the mountain lions that do live on Earth today. Saber-toothed cats had canine teeth that look deadly. Scientists aren't sure what purpose the oversized teeth served. The large cats may have chased prey animals into the tar.

A painting of what a saber-toothed cat catching a ground sloth may have looked like

The mastodon is one of the largest animals that lived in southern California. It looks a lot like a small elephant. Some of the pits may have had a layer of water over the tar. Mastodons that stepped into the pool for a drink may have gotten trapped in the tar.

A painting of what a mastodon may have looked like

A mastodon fossil skeleton

Why did the saber-toothed cat, mastodon, and ground sloth become extinct? It's not because they all fell into the tar pits. Only a few were trapped in the tar and died. Organisms become extinct when the environment changes.

In southern California, the climate was warming up after the *ice ages*. When the environment changed, some animals thrived, some animals looked for other places to live, and some died. The animals that are known only as *fossils* from the La Brea tar pits could not survive in the changed environment.

GLOSSARY

Cotyledon The "seed leaf" that provides the germinated seed with food.

Crayfish A freshwater animal that has a hard shell and prominent pincers.

Crustacean A class of mostly aquatic animals with hard, flexible shells, jointed legs, and two pairs of antennae.

Embryo The undeveloped plant within a seed.

Environment The surroundings of a plant or animal.

Exoskeleton The hard outer covering of some animals that supports and protects them.

Extinct No longer alive anywhere on Earth.

Fossil A part of a plant or animal that lived long ago and has turned to rock.

Fruit A structure of a plant in which seeds are found.

Germination The beginning of development of a seed after a period of dormancy or rest.

Habitat Where an organism naturally lives.

Hydroponics Growing plants without soil in a water-based nutrient solution.

Ice age A time in the history of Earth when large sheets of ice covered much of the northern half of the planet.

Life cycle The sequence of changes undergone by an organism as it develops from its earliest stage to the same stage in the next generation.

Molting The process by which crayfish shed their outer shells in order to grow.

Nutrient A material used by a living organism to help it grow and develop.

Parasite An organism that lives on or in a plant or animal of a different kind. The parasite gets nutrients from the other animal or plant.

Predator An animal that hunts and catches other animals for food.

Reproduce To produce new plants or new animals.

Root The part of a plant that grows downward in the soil. Roots provide support and take up water and nutrients.

Seed The structure in a fruit that holds the undeveloped plant, or embryo.

Seed coat The outer covering of a seed.

Stem Any stalk supporting leaves, flowers, or fruit.

Structure Any identifiable part of an organism.

Thrive To grow fast and stay healthy.